WATCH THEM
• • • • • • •
GROW!

# The Life Cycle of a
# CHICKEN

**Shaye Reynolds**

**PowerKiDS**
press™

New York

Published in 2016 by The Rosen Publishing Group, Inc.
29 East 21st Street, New York, NY 10010

First Edition

Editor: Caitie McAneney
Book Design: Reann Nye

Photo Credits: Cover spiro/Shutterstock.com; p. 5 Catalin Petolea/Shutterstock.com; pp. 7, 23 (eggs) ddsign/Shutterstock.com; p. 9 thieury/Shutterstock.com; p. 10 kmlsphotos/Thinkstockphotos.com; p. 13 Anneka/Shutterstock.com; pp. 15, 23 (chick), 24 (down) Goncharuk Maksim/Shutterstock.com; pp. 16, 23 (chick eating) eurobanks/Shutterstock.com; pp. 18, 24 (comb, wattle) Cherkas/Shutterstock.com; p. 21 Art_man/Shutterstock.com; p. 23 (hen) Zelenenka Yuliia/Shutterstock.com.

Library of Congress Cataloging-in-Publication Data

Reynolds, Shaye, author.
 The life cycle of a chicken / Shaye Reynolds.
     pages cm. — (Watch them grow!)
 Includes index.
 ISBN 978-1-4994-0664-1 (pbk. book)
 ISBN 978-1-4994-0665-8 (6 pack)
 ISBN 978-1-4994-0666-5 (library binding)
 1. Chickens—Life cycles—Juvenile literature. I. Title.
 SF487.5.R49 2016
 636.5—dc23
                                        2014048535

Manufactured in the United States of America

CPSIA Compliance Information: Batch #WS15PK: For Further Information contact Rosen Publishing, New York, New York at 1-800-237-9932

# Contents

A chicken's body changes as it grows. These changes make up a chicken's life cycle.

A chicken is a bird. All birds start inside eggs.

A female chicken is called a hen. Hens lay eggs.

A hen sits on her eggs
to keep them warm.

A baby chicken grows inside its egg until it's big enough. Then, it breaks out of the egg.

13

A baby chicken is called a chick. It has soft feathers called **down**.

A chick eats bugs and seeds.
It grows fast.

comb →

← wattle

18

A chick grows a **wattle** under its chin. It grows a **comb** on its head.

A chick grows bigger until it's an adult. Male chicks become roosters.

Female chicks become hens. They can lay eggs. The life cycle starts all over again!

# Life Cycle of a Chicken

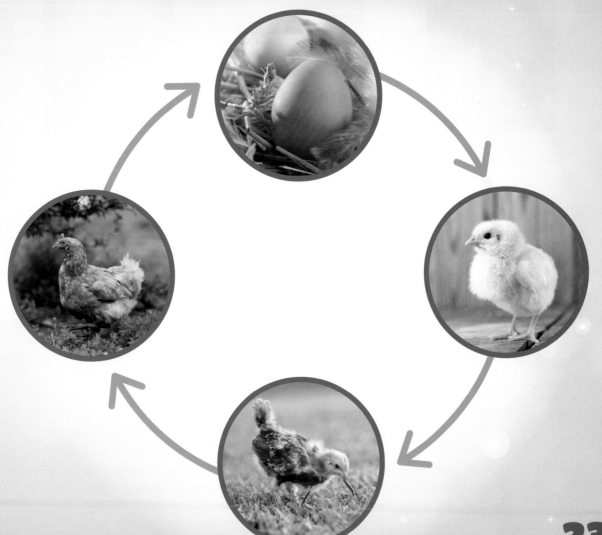

# Words to Know

comb

down

wattle

# Index

# Websites

Due to the changing nature of Internet links, PowerKids Press has developed an online list of websites related to the subject of this book. This site is updated regularly. Please use this link to access the list: www.powerkidslinks.com/wtg/chic